MW01229415

ARCHANGELOLOGY SANDALPHON HARMONY

IF YOU CALL THEM THEY WILL COME

KIM CALDWELL

A Division of Archangelology LLC

https://archangelology.com

Introduction Editing and enhancement Rachel Caldwell

Book Editing Grammarly

ISBN: 978-1-947284-33-3

Book Cover Picture Nicola Zalewski

Cover design Kim Caldwell

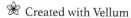 Created with Vellum

1

ABOUT THE SERIES

"Logic will get you from point A to B. Imagination will take you everywhere."-- Einstein

This Archangelology book and the entire series aim to lift the reader one step at a time. You may read this piece anytime you desire Upliftment and want to feel good now, never underestimate the power of feeling good for creating more of what you want.

Choose this or any of the other Archangelology Books or Matching Audios to read or listen to for at least 44 nights and raise your vibration consistently for an Uplifted Feeling and Life.

This piece is one of a series of Angelic Upgrade books that fill you with Divine Angelic codes. Angelic laws are based on love and light and thus, operate for free-will, so we must call and ask the Archangels for help.

When working with your book relax, take deep breaths and ground to Mother Earth. Focus on Intentions for whatever it is your heart desires that are for the highest good of all involved. Intentions for these energies that we can not see but feel when we are ready. There are those that believe The Archangels are the Ones that make Law of Attraction Work.

This series of books take on a life of its own as the Archangels move and play from book to book, creating a Delicious Alchemy. Each book becomes an instrument in this Celestial Symphony for a more fulfilling life. Many of the Archangel books also carry and infuse the Violet Flame and Divine Connection to Mother Earth for a transformational experience.

Each book has a matching meditation audio available for your listening pleasure at https://archangelology.com. Please visit our site for your gifts. The book and the audio have similar wording, yet according to the Angels, they Upgrade us differently. Each medium has a unique experience, energetically Upgrading us in distinct ways. Each time you read or hear an Archangel Upgrade, a new dimension is added or adjusted for your benefit.

Become interactive with your book; when inspired, read the words aloud, and let them roll over you, feeling the love and magic that the Angels radiate. When inspired create your own rituals; there is no right or wrong way. As you play with the rock stars of the Celestial realm, you can expect your life to become more heavenly, more peaceful.

You may Notice Many Words are Uniquely Capitalized throughout this series; this is yet another way the Angels infuse us. When you see this try to feel that word or phrase; sensing the depth of its Intensity of Pure Divine Light throughout your Being.

The Archangel Energy is neither male

nor female. This gender fluidity is made clear in this series by the use of the word they or he/she speak to convey a non-gender energy that shifts roles to uplift and nurture you. The upgrades happen in Divine Time, and there is no schedule. There is no competition. There is no rush. Wherever you are in the process is perfect.

A word about the length of this book. "Less is more." This Series of books is the result of decades of study in the art of Law of Attraction, Angelic knowing and energy healing, condensed here for you in a format that will shift and benefit the reader. If you found your way here, you can expect miracles. As Einstein said, "There are only two ways to live your life. One is as though nothing is a miracle. The other is as though everything is a miracle." The matching audio to this book is 44 minutes, so working with that is always an option.

Both Neville Goddard and Albert Einstein stated that our imagination is the creative force. Goddard went so far as to imply that our imagination is the God/dess Energy. I mention this to you because as you read these words with much more than your eyes, let your imagination run wild with vivid pictures of the love the magical Archangels have for you and of your adventures together. Enjoy.

2

ABOUT ARCHANGEL SANDALPHON

~

Meet Archangel Sandalphon! She/He serves to transmit Our prayers and desires to the God/dess energy. In addition to serving as a means of connection to the Divine, Sandalphon is also the Archangel of Harmony and Music. Sandalphon facilitates in strengthening our connection to Mother Earth and aligns us with her/his balancing energy. Archangel Sanfalphon also shows us how singing to our Angels allows us to bolster our connection to Celestial gifts. Archangels Metatron, Zadkiel, Haniel, Jophiel, Raphael, Camael, Uriel,

Gabriel, and Raziel all direct us on our respective paths towards alignment, joy, and blessings. In this Divine Angelic Alchemy you can experience flying through Inner-Earth like a superhero. Travel to the higher dimensions of love, light, and peace with the assistance of the Archangels. Feel the Archangels' singing voices and enjoy the resultant feelings of bliss and tranquility that inundate your being. Moreover, Sandalphon reminds us how advantageous practicing neutrality and nonjudgment is for the purpose of cultivating a more peaceful and happy life. She/He also empowers us with the tools to create new beginnings of joy. Focusing on these practices will help you shift and refresh your consciousness towards that of a magnet for confidence, peace, and prosperity. Spending time with Archangels creates a heavenly life. The information I have put together is meant to work for your individualized wants and needs. It is not a prescribed set of general steps or rules, but rather it aims to help you in your particular journey and give you what you need to begin or grow in a mindset. You may read a sentence, a paragraph, or the whole book. It's just whatever you feel you need to embark on this Celestial journey to a more abundant life. There is no wrong or right way to use this tool. The only thing I recommend you keep in the forefront of your practice is to ensure you are enjoying the process. Meet one of the Archangels in the Archangelology Book and Audio Series that is here to help you at this time. If you call Archangel Sandalphon, she/he will come, just as all of the Archangels will come to your assistance when beckoned. For gifts from the Archangels visit https://archangelology.com.

3

ARCHANGEL SANDALPHON
HARMONY

~

Archangelology. Sandalphon. Archangel Sandalphon is the Archangel who takes our prayers straight to the God/dess Source, who connects us with that Divine Energy. Archangels can get our prayers answered and help us in times of need. Archangel Sandalphon is also the Archangel of music and of connecting to Mother Earth.

Archangel Sandalphon wants to take us on a Divine Journey now to help us have more connection and more bliss and remember how to connect to the music of the Universe. Deep healing breath.

Say with me now: "Archangel Sandalphon, please come into my life. Please help me and take my prayers straight to the God/dess Energy. Please help me remember to connect with high vibrational music and sound more often, to calm me and heal me." Thank you, Archangel Sandalphon, thank you. Deep healing breath.

Now Archangel Sandalphon appears right before you, yes. She/He gazes upon you with such love and knowing. Remember the Archangel energy is neither male nor female. It is the Divine Combination of both with the God/dess energy. Archangel Sandalphon takes your hand and starts to guide you. It's a beautiful sunny day. The air is crisp and fresh. The sun is bright and beaming upon you, and you feel it invigorating your mind, body, and spirit. As Archangel Sandalphon walks right beside you, you're amazed by the grace and beauty of her/his being. You glide together.

There are greenery and beautiful, bright grass all around you. You see mountains. You see beautiful trees. You feel your heart connecting with Mother Earth. Archangel Sandalphon gently, melodically speaks to you and reminds you to connect to Mother Earth and the heaven. To see a beautiful beam of light starting from the core of Mother Earth and beaming up at you, take a deep breath. This Divine Energy flows all out through your center, stabilizing you, balancing you, and goes up into the heaven. Take a deep, healing breath.

Feel your balance, feel the tingles, feel the bliss as you start to glow and your vibration starts to raise. As you feel your vibration start to build and the beautiful Archangel Sandalphon standing right beside you, you notice a pathway with stepping stones, and you start to walk towards a beautiful cave, and as you do, you relax and count these stepping stones.

One, step again; watch the stones. Two, they are vibrating with a translucent color. Three. they seem to come alive under your feet. Four. as your vibration rises higher and higher. Five. as you feel your connection to all that is. Six. as you remember your connection and your power. Seven, eight, nine. Take a deep healing breath. Ten. yes.

As you feel completely relaxed – at peace and blissful ease – you see the cave entrance, and Archangel Sandalphon lets you know that you're going to take a magnificent journey. Sandalphon takes your arm to steady you, as you are as steady as you can be, and you look about in this cavern, this cave, and it's covered with the most Divine Crystals, sparkling – sparkling, healing amethyst crystals. Take a deep healing breath. Look around; the walls are sparkling, beautiful, beautiful healing crystals, and you feel so invigorated, so alive, so blissful, and so happy, and as you look up, you smile at Archangel Sandalphon.

He smiles back at you, and he telepathically lets you know, you are going on a journey to the inner Earth. Your energy rises; you feel so blissful and happy. You've heard about the beautiful inner Earth and that it exists. You relax, and you follow the path. The caves, you go deeper and deeper into the tunnels, you go deeper and deeper along with Archangel Sandalphon. Archangel

Sandalphon energizes and infuses you with the knowledge that you are completely safe and that you are about to embark upon a world that you have only imagined and now it is going to come to life with and for you. Deep healing breath.

Sandalphon takes your hand as you both gently start to float through the cavern, through the caves, and you start to move more quickly now, and you swim, and you glide. You are holding Archangel Sandalphon's hand, and you are feeling light as a feather. You are feeling high on delicious, fresh Inner Earth air. You see the crystals sparkling, you feel their energy infusing you, and you start to notice flying beside you, beautiful, beautiful little humming-birds, at least they look like hummingbirds.

You've never seen anything quite like them before. They're tiny, and they make beautiful little songs. Archangel Sandalphon explains to you that these beautiful little creatures raise your vibration and you simply need to call them. You feel better as they start to come closer to you and your body starts to tingle and vibrate. These are beautiful, beautiful little birds whose wings move so fast that you can't see the movement and you can feel the vibrations all around you, and you feel your vibrations rising, and rising, and you smile. On your other side, you see Archangel Michael, standing and supporting you. Michael is the Archangel of protection. Michael is here to help you feel safe on your journey. Michael lets you know that anytime you need him, simply call, "Michael, Michael, Michael," and sing to your Angel. Archangel Sandalphon gives you the same message; anytime you would like Archangel Sandalphon, simply sing, "Archangel Sandalphon, Archangel Sandalphon, Sandalphon."

Yes, and you are floating and flying with these beautiful Angelic Celestial Beings, and the beautiful tiny hummingbirds that are surreal. The whole scene feels surreal to you, and you take a deep healing breath, and you feel your vibration rising and rising. Archangel Sandalphon explains to you that one of her/his gifts is that of music and that listening to music is just as important as creating music and it is a Divine Interaction

Much of the music that we love and listen to, we have helped to create.

As you read to this book, realize that you have contributed to creating it, the collective consciousness together, creating. Archangel Sandalphon reminds you to sing to your Angels, to sing with Divine Music, and then raise your vibration, and lift your vibration up to higher dimensions. Sandalphon reminds you that the Earth – the Goddess Mother Earth – is now moving up to higher vibrations. This means that love, peace, light, and Divine Intentions are the reasons why our world is raising in consciousness. The days, of competition, and fears are sliding away.

Archangel Sandalphon reminds you when you go into fear, take a deep breath, listen to your breathing, hear the melody of your breathing, and then, if you can sing, sing to your Angels. Sing with me now, "Archangel Metatron, Archangel Zadkiel, Archangel Haniel, Archangel Jophiel, Archangel Raphael, Archangel Camael, Archangel Uriel, Archangel Gabriel, Archangel Raziel, Archangel Orion."

Sing to these beings and call them. All these beautiful beings have their books and audios in the Archangelology Series. Feel free to play with them anytime you like. Take a deep healing breath. As you continue to fly and soar through the caves, it feels spacious. It feels expanded. The energy feels completely different from what you would expect when you are in a cave. It feels like you have all the room in the world. It feels like your heart is expanding and connecting with Mother Earth. It feels like you're getting closer and closer to Mother Earth. It feels like you can feel her heartbeat, her pulse, and you keep traveling, and you keep moving.

Archangel Sandalphon and Archangel Michael telepathically let you know that you are doing great. You look like a superhero flying through the caves quickly, with courage, with faith and that you know exactly where you're going. Yes, you are moving into higher and higher dimensions. As we come into the fifth dimension, 5D.

As we fly out of the last turn, we find ourselves in the middle of the gigantic beautiful inner Earth. Deep healing breath. We're now in the fifth dimension. We're now in the center of Mother Earth. How exciting, and we have Archangel Sandalphon with us. We're connected to our Mother Earth. We also have Archangel Michael with us who is our protector. We are perfectly safe.

We notice ahead there is a beautiful, glowing light, so we follow it and go that way, and we come upon a waterfall. Deep healing breath. We stop at this waterfall to take a break. Archangel Sandalphon lets you know that you might want to go up under the waterfall now and enjoy a wonderful, refreshing, relaxing treatment. You walk along stones and pebbles. They are in beautiful bright colors. They seem to glow from within now. You come upon and stand directly under this waterfall, and to your delight, there is light shimmering down from the waterfall. You feel the light come down upon your body.

The light is changing colors. You can feel it raising your vibration and making you tingle. You see a bright, brilliant violet light and water falling upon your body. You feel it taking off layer after layer any stress, layers of any negative emotion, just being gently washed off you with this beautiful healing light that you've never seen before that feels like love. The light pours down upon you, and this lovely violet color makes your skin tingle. You smile, and you look up, and you touch your face, and you touch your hair, and you let the cleansing light fall upon you.

You take a deep healing breath, and you feel all the cares of the world washing away now. You hear in the background all the Angels that we called singing a melodious song surrounding you as you stand under this beautiful waterfall and you are just shimmered out with violet light. Then, you notice the light start to change color. It turns to white; the light comes down upon you and sparkles on you. Any heavy feelings of guilt or shame seem to disappear from you now. Yes, you start to feel amazing.

Your mind starts to go into white peaceful pureness. The only thing you can think of is love, how loved you are, and how much the beautiful Angels love you. How much they want to help you. You look over, and Archangel Michael and Archangel

Sandalphon are standing, waiting for you, so lovingly, so kind, and so nurturing. They both telepathically let you know that you're never alone, that you have a strong team behind you, beside you, before you.

They walk before you to let you know when you need to take a left for a great happy day or to let you know the best course of action to take. Yes, your Angels are all around you, supporting you, loving you. Then, you notice that the light turns a beautiful aqua blue and the light shimmers down upon you with the waterfall, and you feel your back relaxing; you feel like the weight of the world is being washed off your back, and you start to feel fear leave your body. You feel all the fear just draining out into the inner Earth, and you look around, and the whole inner Earth is glowing.

You feel the heartbeat of Mother Earth. As you connect with her, you hear her messages, and Sandalphon smiles at you as she/he watches you smile when you get these messages. Mother Earth says to you, "We are connected. You are my children. I support you. I love you." As you send love back to me, you help to heal Mother Earth, the whole planet." Deep healing breath.

You feel this love radiating from Mother Earth, and you know, you know that this connection is real and you know that you'll support and love your Mother Earth more and more. Deep healing breath. Now you watch as the next color soothes and comes down on you too. It's a beautiful red color, and it flashes down upon you, and you start to feel energized. Now we're going to practice how to let all heavy emotions fall in and be transmuted. Archangel Jophiel walks up. Archangel Jophiel smiles at you and lets you know that all you need to do is call on your Archangels any time you feel like things are bogging you down. If there are entities, or there's a ghost, or there's anything around you that's no longer for your highest good, call your Archangels and ask them. Ask them to take these entities to the light. Ask them to take these ghosts to the light. Do not fear these entities; just call for help and know it is coming. When we fear anything it gives it power, practice your Ho'oponopono to make amazing shifts. Simply say, "I love you, I am sorry, Please forgive me, I forgive you. Thank you" over and over till you feel the shift that is going to happen.

Now we're going to do an exercise. Wherever you're sitting, you're going to ask that Archangel Michael and Archangel Raphael to create a light door, and usher these beings through this door to the light. They're going to create a light door, and right now, while you're under this beautiful, wonderful waterfall, observe as any negative beings, negative entities, or ghosts leave your environment. Take a deep healing breath.

Archangel Michael is with you, and Archangel Raphael is with you; ask them to help these entities or beings go to the light and do it with love. It is all love. There's no need to be afraid of them. Just ask for this to be done now. Yes, and as it's being done, just feel the light washing away anything that no longer serves you. Watch as the light turns to a beautiful soothing aqua sea foam green, and this green light washes down upon you. Yes, you have your Archangel Michael and your Archangel Metatron and your Archangel Raphael and your Archangel

Jophiel all surrounding around and supporting you.

You notice as they all put their hands together and create a circle of light around you, yes. Take a deep healing breath as they create a golden tube of light, and you feel your energy tingling, and you can feel everything being cleaned and cleared. Now we will set the intention and ask, "Archangel Sandalphon, please help to clear and clean my energy. Help it to feel bright and amazing. Help to remove anything that no longer needs to be there. Help my vibration to rise, to go higher and higher, and help my vibration stay in the higher dimensions as often as possible and help me stay grounded to the glorious Mother Earth." Deep healing breath.

As you do this, you see you and the Archangel start to vibrate so fast that you turn a tube of golden light. This golden light goes straight up to the heavens. Deep healing breath. Yes. As that light goes all the way up to the heaven, Archangel Sandalphon lets you know that this is you connecting to your Source Energy more strongly than ever.

come more easily. We appear to be in a calmer state. As we practice this, as we practice our neutrality, each moment can be a new beginning.

As we focus our minds on all the blessings, on the higher dimensions, and on the beautiful sacred light geometry that exists all around us, things become more joyful, more blissful. As we count our blessings and remember how truly, truly blessed we are, we return to being an Earth Angel. As we Activate the miracle of forgiveness, as we forgive ourselves first and foremost, and then allow ourselves to forgive others, we become the light worker, the peaceful being we're meant to be. Peace and harmony become the way.

As we go and stay into neutrality, our spiritual gifts activate more and more. Take a deep healing breath. Yes, you are a Divine Master; you have many spiritual gifts, and as we learn to work with them, we learn to raise our vibration, we learn to open our hearts and honor our beauty, and we stay connected to the Divine. Take a deep healing breath. You truly are an Earth Angel.

Now, Sandalphon takes your hand, and

you start to take your journey back to upper Earth. Sandalphon wants you to know that you're going to take this wonderful raised vibration with you, and you're going to take it with you, everywhere you go, so that you can experience the Earth on the higher dimensions more and more often. When you're not at the higher vibrations, we relax, and we know that we will, with the help of the Archangels, get back there in Divine Timing.

We start to float and start to move back through the caves effortlessly, easily. We notice beautiful, shimmering crystals as we move back. We notice a lot of clear crystals and rose quartz crystals for love. As we pass these crystals, they're charging us with love, with light, with peace. We notice emerald crystals in the cavern. These emerald crystals are charging our vibration with health and vitality. We notice turquoise stones in the ground. The turquoise stones fill us with well-being.

We notice gorgeous labradorite crystals. Labradorite crystals keep us in a great mood. Make us feel better, make us feel happy. We notice as these crystals seem to be transforming us, filling us with light. We feel like we're soaring, and we notice as our beautiful little hummingbirds start to fly with us again, continuously raising our vibration, and feel guided.

Archangel Michael appears beside you, so you feel so protected. You're flying and enjoying your journey, and you come to the exit of the cave, and you come out and emerge. You emerge transformed. You emerge filled with light and love. Filled with song, the Earth, and Mother Earth's beauty, and it's evening, and you walk over to a beautiful clearing. There's an emerald-green expansion of grass, and Archangel Sandalphon leads you there.

Archangel Sandalphon wants to give you an ancient knowing that you can use in your daily life. Archangel Sandalphon reminds you that when you sing to your Angels, they can hear you. They can feel your vibration, and you can sing to them, and then, of course, you can let them know exactly what you want help with. It also helps to write it down. If you see yourself igniting with lightning, the Angels see that too. Archangel

Sandalphon whispers in your ear to sing to Archangel Raziel. Sing with me now. "Archangel Raziel, Archangel Raziel, Archangel Raziel," and appearing before you is Archangel Raziel, the Archangel of Wisdom in all her/his glory.

Next Archangel Sandalphon whispers into your ear melodically. It's time to call Archangel Gabriel. "Archangel Gabriel." Sing this with me now, call the Archangel of Hope. "Archangel Gabriel, Archangel Gabriel, Archangel Gabriel." And right before you appears Archangel Gabriel, the Archangel of Hope. Next, Archangel Sandalphon reminds you to call on Archangel Uriel, the Archangel of peace. Sing with me now, "Archangel Uriel, Archangel Uriel, Archangel Uriel." At that exact moment appears Archangel Uriel.

Archangel Uriel, filling you with peaceful bliss. Next, Archangel Sandalphon whispers in your ear to call Archangel Camael. Sing with me now, "Archangel Camael, Archangel Camael, Archangel Camael." Archangel Camael is the Archangel of courage and strength to help you make it through as beautiful Divine Sparkles of light infuse you. Infusing you with bliss, infusing you with neutrality, infusing you with your connection to the Earth, infusing you with Divine Love. Infusing you with health and abundance. Take a deep, healing breath.

You notice as Violet Flames start to wrap around you and all your Angels. The flames lift up and up, and you hold out your hands in front of you and notice the beautiful Violet Flames coming from your palms. You feel such serene bliss as you realize and remember that you are a vessel of love, of light, of the Violet Flame. You feel this as your Angels all start to sing to you together, and Archangel Sandalphon stands right in front of you, smiling upon you with such sweet Divine Melodic Energy.

This moves all throughout your body, and your mind and your body and your spirit merge with Archangel Sandalphon in her/his amazing, beautiful song. This is the song of joy. This is the song of bliss. This is the song of our Mother Earth rising into higher dimensions. This is our song of light and love and peace and happiness. Sing with me now.

Feel your song, feel the melody of your heart. Feel as you become the heart-centered being that you are, as we become the new humans along with our beautiful Archangels, as we step into our world as Earth Angels. Deep healing breath.

The songs of the Angels are swirling around you, filling you with confidence, with knowing, with remembering exactly who you are, a Divine God/dess here in physical form. Thank you. Thank you, Archangel Sandalphon. Thank you, Archangels. Thank you, Divine Beings of Light. Thank you.

4

BONUS CHAPTER MUSIC'S
DIVINE NATURE

From the Book and Audio Program *Activate Your Abundance* By Kim Caldwell, available at Archangelologydotcom

MUSIC'S DIVINE NATURE

"Music washes away from the soul the dust of everyday life." ---Berthold Auerbach

Inspiring music can automatically put us in a state of bliss and peace. When we find music that appeals to us personally, we can lift our mind and spirits to a lovely state. There is a vibrational healing taking place on deep levels, a connection to Divine forces we cannot see but feel at the core of our being.

Consciously use music for lifting and creating on new levels. As we listen to beautiful music, take note of the deep chords being struck in our being. I am always in awe of how profoundly the right music can lift and touch my inner world. Divine energy is flowing freely through, clearing all the blocks. Of course, everyone will have different music that moves them. Look for music that lifts and inspires you. Music is so personal. Learn to use music to bring a sense of joy and enthusiasm to your life.

When I hear one of my favorite singers Donna De Lory sing the beautiful chant Lokah Samasta Sukhino Bhavantu, which means may all beings be happy and free and may my life be a giving to this happiness and freedom for all, I get lifted to new heights each time. Certain music delivers a message and vibration of peace and well-being beyond compare.

We can use music to calm us.

Each morning I love to start my day with a beautiful walk in nature. For me, uplifting music is a must. I take deep breaths as the Divine beat helps me move with ease and joy. I am typing this book as soothing music plays and connects me with my God/dess source, allowing this information to flow. As the tone and beat plays, Divine ideas flow to and through me.Music has the ability to make us feel and lift that is beyond words or explanation.

Singing and humming have a very uplifting effect on the body, mind and spirit. Chanting is practiced with calming and centering effects in many religions. I was blessed to meet a yoga master who practiced chanting and yoga for decades. He explained that it is not the meaning of the words that create the benefits. millions of people receive from chanting daily. Actually, it is the vibration of sound in the throat. The vibration soothes and lifts the whole individual, clearing and healing our energy centers. Chanting actually heals the body on many and deep levels. In my humble opinion, singinghappily has the same positive effect. Try it; sing with a light, happy heart a song you really love and experience lifted states.

When practice on a consistent basis, you can expect to feel better consistently. A perfect example of this is how children often sing happily and stay in a great place.

The applications of music to enhance our lives are endless; as we take advantage of this, we are lifted to new heights.

5

ANGELIC HABITS

There is a saying that our habits make us who we are.

The habit of calling in our Angels creates more peace and poise. As we stop, take a deep breath and call our Angels, this is an opportunity to ground into the now moment and, if we are really on our game, also ground into our beautiful mother earth.

Calling our Angels takes practice and forethought it is a wonderful way to calm fear or anxiety. Acknowledging this Angelic Support allows us to see perceived "challenges" as opportunities. Reminding us that we are never alone and are supported by the

Celestial Masters, the Archangels, and much more.

Make reminders for yourself in convenient places where you will see them stop, breathe and call your Angels.

Do you have an event coming up? Call your Angels now and let them line things up smoothly for you. Allow the Divine Intelligence of the universe to help you.

Please be patient with yourself and with your Angels. Let attachment to outcome go, and as they say, "go with the flow."

Please remember that Angels are on Divine Time, so let go of when you think things "should happen" and allow yourself to relax. Play with this and have fun just like you did as a kid. You can do it and enjoy the process.

6

ANGELIC MANIFESTATION
JOURNAL BONUS

Create more of the life you want with the Archangels as you explore and focus with your Angelic Journal. If you are ready, let's set intentions now to make your Archangel Michael Book a Manifestation tool. It is said that humans have so many thoughts going on in our heads at once that it is hard for Angels and Spirit Guides to hear what we want help with. This is one of the many reasons it is so powerful to get very clear on what we desire and write it out in a designated journal for our Archangels. This way, they can understand our needs better and help us with our dreams and goals in Divine Time.

It has been proven that when we write things down, more of what we desire comes to us. Goals get accomplished, and things flow with more ease. Adding the Amazing Archangels to your journaling just makes the results that much stronger. As we set intentions for what we want and take the time to focus and write it down in our journal, unseen forces move on our behalf. We are going to enlist the help of this Divine Knowing with our Archangel book in an interactive way and turn our book into a manifestation tool. We are also going to play with our books like children and have some fun. Children are powerful creators, and we will take on some of their great habits for their creative value.

Focus and underline ideas you resonate with in your book and become immersed in Upliftment. There is a deeper connection as we become interactive with our Archangel books. We may get colored pens and underline areas of our book that feel important or special to us. We may want to draw pictures of desired blessings or anything that makes us feel good. We may want to mark different areas of our book with hearts, stars, or Angel wings. Get sticky tab notes, a personal favorite, and stick them to your favorite pages you want to return to often. In your journal section, place a sticky tab on an area you want to let the Angels know to help you write in and as a personal reminder. Let your Angelic interaction and intuition guide you with what feels best. Neville Goddard and Albert Einstein both explained that our imagination is a creative force and can bring great blessings to our lives. We will bring our imagination fully into our process now. You may want to add stickers to enhance pages. Place a beautiful angel or magic looking card in your book as a bookmark. Get creative and give your book some personal character. Putting clover or flowers in your book to press and dry, adds some powerful nature magic to your process. Roses are a great choice as they have the highest vibration of any flower. You may give lovely flowers as an offering to your Archangels as well. Giving back is always a beneficial activity.

Everyone has magical abilities. Some of us know this, and some do not. My point is all these ideas are simple and will work for anyone who puts forth an effort and has the faith to relax and let go so the angels may do their work. Of course, anything we put out comes back to us, so we want to always include "for the highest good" in all requests.

In all my studies of magical herbs, cinnamon is found in many different traditions for enhancement of all things wanted and removing things not wanted. You may want to rub a dab of cinnamon mixed with a touch of olive oil on your journal in an intentional shape such as a heart for more love or the infinity symbol for more abundance. Then say to yourself, "I anoint my journal with success and happiness with the help of the Archangels." Anointment has been practiced for eons with much luck and advancement. Basil and Sage could just as easily be utilized. Anything that feels magical and speaks to you in your spice cabinet most likely has wonderful magical properties. Use these gifts of nature with intention and focus for a more joyous life. The idea is to create a magnet for all you desire that is for your highest good with your Archangel Journal.

You may want to underline ideas in colors that mean something to you. The sky is the limit, get creative and juicy with your book, knowing that amazing things are being created.

Next, we have dedicated pages that are waiting for you to fill them with your heart's desires that Michael will help you achieve as long as they are for the highest good. You may write anything you want in your Archangel Journal. There is no right or wrong way to do this. You may ask the Archangels to help you release things from your life, share your hopes and dreams, or ask questions. I love to ask my angels questions and patiently wait to know they will lead me to the answer in Divine Time. Be open and honest with your journaling and the Archangels understanding that the only ones who need to see your Angel Journal are you and your Angels. Keeping your wishes to yourself is very powerful for manifesting as well.

We have created categories for you, and

of course, there will Be freestyle areas, so play with this and have fun. After you play with your journal, you may put it away in a sacred space knowing all is in Divine Order. Remember, magic works just in its own time and asking where the results are will only block things, so relax, have faith, and patience. You may come back to read your Archangel book and add more to it at any time. Know that unseen beneficial forces are moving to help you now and forevermore. Play with and collect other Archangelology books and audios, remembering, "If you call them, they will come." Check out the Archangelology Archangel Journaling Book for more ideas on taking your Journaling Process to the next "celestial" level. The Archangels have tied this whole series Together for us in such a Divinely Intelligent way. Spend time in nature with your book, filling it with love, imagination, and Angelic magic for exponential results. You are a powerful creator and loved by all that is.

Write on the blank areas of your book and on the lined journal areas. Think

222

8

CALL ARCHANGEL SANDALPHON TO SEE YOUR WORLD FROM A "BIRDS EYE VIEW"

As we evolve and enlighten, there are times when we can get so into our Highest Self that we can soar like an Angel above all the conditions and problems of the world and get a deep knowing that things will work out even better than we could have imagined. Journal about all the ways you can do this here creatively with Archangel Sandalphon, St. Rita, and the Blue Flame Angels. Feel your power now and expound on it in your journal. If inspired, add a smudge of one of your magical power oils and let it simmer here with all this Divine Angel Magic.

10

CALL FOR DIVINE WISDOM WITH ARCHANGEL SANDALPHON, ARCHANGEL RAZIEL AND THE BLUE FLAME ANGELS

Call on Archangel Sandalphon to help you connect to your highest self with the help of the Blue Flame Angels. Visualize as Archangel Sandalphon stands on one side of you, shimmering you with rainbow angel sparkles to your third eye. At the same time, Archangel Raziel, the Archangel of wisdom, stands behind you, shimmering you with Divine Sapphire Angel Wisdom Sparkles. Feel as you connect while the Blue Flame Angels surround you all in a circle. Let your imagination spark as you journal about all the miracles you create due to this powerful process.

11

SING AND JOURNAL WITH
YOUR ANGELS

Feel as Archangel Sandalphon and The Blue Flame angels shimmer you with more Bliss. Smile as cherub Angels sing your Praises. Journal how it feels to be loved and supported by such Divine Beings. Feel as Angelic Harmony radiates all around you and charges you with more well-being.

Remember how to connect to the music of the Universe now. Draw symbols and bring your colored markers to this page.

12

CONNECT TO MOTHER EARTH AND FEEL MORE HEAVEN ON EARTH

Visualize standing barefoot on the earth with Archangel Sandalphon holding your hand. Walk in the lush, soft green grass as sparkles of light shimmer from your feet, connecting you more to Mother Earth. Feel as the Blue Flame Angels join, dismantling anything non-beneficial and creating space for more Harmony. Write all the Harmony and Bliss you feel as you connect more often to your Angels.

13

MOTHER MARY AND ARCHANGEL SANDALPHON MOTHERING SUPPORT

Take a deep, slow breath and feel as Archangel Sandalphon appears beside you. On your other side, smile as you see the Divine Mother Mary appear. Smile and visualize these magnificent beings shimmering you with Divine Feminine Energies to help you feel loved and supported. List all the ways this mothering energy can assist you. Call upon these Divine Beings anytime you would like more mothering support in your life.

14

FEEL ARCHANGEL SANDALPHON LIFT YOUR VIBRATIONS WITH ARCHANGEL MICHAEL

Call Archangel Michael, the Archangel of protection, now to come into your life with Archangel Sandalphon and create Archangel Alchemy all around you and your entire circle of influence. Visualize as both of these mighty Angels shimmer you with rainbow angel sparkles throughout your space. Allow this feeling to raise your vibration and bring a blissful smile to your heart. Journal new inspired ideas this brings you, and feel free to add magical pictures and oils.

15

CALL IN MORE FREEDOM WITH THE BLUE FLAME ANGELS AND ARCHANGEL SANDALPHON

Feel freedom on deep levels as you call The Blue Flame Angels to remove any sinister energies from your life and your world. Send the Blue Flame Angels out into your world to remove and refresh. Ask Archangel Sandalphon to help you write songs of freedom. Sing your songs of freedom to yourself or aloud with your Angels. **As you call the Angels, the sky is the limit on how much Freedom and Heaven on Earth the Angels can help you bring in. You are that powerful, and as you bring these Divine Angels to the Earth plane, you are such a gift. Thank you.** Hear all the

Angels singing your Praises. Write out all the Divine messages you get.

More information on how Calling Angels Blesses the world in the book Ascended Masters. Ascended Masters Speak on Angels (Saint Germain Foundation Printing.)

MORE ANGEL IDEAS

16

SING YOUR WISHES WITH ST. RITA AND ARCHANGEL SANDALPHON

Sing to St. Rita, the Saint of granting Wishes, and Archangel Sandalphon. Write out lovely songs about any wishes you would like to have help fulfill while being happy where you are. Smile while you visualize the gorgeous St. Rita in brilliant technicolor dancing to your beautiful songs and helping you and Archangel Sandalphon create more blessings. Save this sacred journaling experience and evolve it as inspired.

17

CALL IN AN ARCHANGEL
ORCHESTRA

Visualize Archangel Metatron, the great Archangel of Sacred Geometry, creating and shimmering symbols of Angelic Musical notes with Archangel Sandalphon. See as all these rainbow-colored sacred geometry music note symbols float around you, bringing in more blessings with Archangel Barachiel. Draw pictures in your journal with colored markers to give this angelic vision more depth and creativity. Archangel Gabriel, please assist. Create music symbols for more Peace; Archangel Uriel, please assist. Create music symbols for well-being and fortune; Archangel Raphael, please assist. Create music symbols for more self-love; Archangel Haniel, please assist. Direct this Angelic Orchestra to your Divine benefit. May you always feel your blessings.

18

FEEL THE ARCHANGELS AND ARCHANGEL SANDALPHON LIFTING YOUR VIBRATION WITH SONG

F eel the Archangels lifting your vibration with song. Visualize as Archangel Sandalphon leads a choir of Archangels singing your praises.

See as Archangel Zadkiel sends their Violet Flame Angels all over your world, shimmering the Violet Flame and singing forgiveness. Smile as you see Archangel Orion singing Angelic Magic and Protection throughout your world. Relax as Archangel Uriel sings Angelic Peace throughout your entire circle of influence. Watch as Archangel Barachiel sings Blessings throughout your world. Smile as Archangel Johpiel sings songs that help you Glow. Enjoy as

Archangel Camael sings songs to fill you with Courage and Confidence. Enjoy as Archangel Gabriel sings songs of Hope to and for you. Relax as Archangel Michael sings your song of Security. Watch as the Blue Flame Angels sing Divine Angelic Frequencies that melt anything non-beneficial, creating huge spaces for all these Angelic Blessings. Visualize being in the center of the most magnificent Angelic Flow of Harmony.

19

ACTIVATE YOUR IMAGINATION
ST. LUCY

St. Lucy is the Saint of Seeing the Unseen, which makes her an excellent choice to call in to help ignite your imagination. Visualize St. Lucy sending sparkles of white light to your third eye area right at your forehead to help your imagination create more Heavenly Blessings. Relax as Archangel Sandalphon stands with you, humming Divine Angelic Frequencies to support and lift you. Journal all the beautiful ideas flowing to you.

ADD THE BLUE FLAME ANGELS

C all in the Blue Flame Angels anytime you would like more freedom, peace, blessings, and Heaven on Earth. Write calls and decrees for the Blue Flame Angels, Moon Angels, and Archangels here. Feel the blessings.

You can find information about the Blue Flame Angels here

Ascended Masters. Ascended Masters Speak on Angels (Saint Germain Foundation Printing.)

21

JOURNALING FREEDOM WITH ARCHANGEL ZADKIEL AND THE VIOLET FLAME ANGELS

Call Archangel Zadkiel and the Violet Flame to play with you. You will be creating Archangel Alchemy at its best. You may visualize the Violet Flame as a carpet spreading throughout your world to bring more magic and miracles. You may see the Violet Flame coming from your third eye as you spread it through your world. Get creative with these Divine energies and have fun—Journal all your Violet Flame Blessings.

22

THE BLUE FLAME ANGELS CLEANSE YOUR WORLD

Call in the Blue Flame Angels anytime things that no longer serve us need dismantling. As you play with your Archangels and Saints more, you will be guided to the best times to call these Miracle Workers. St. Philomena is also known as a Miracle Worker, so call on her as well. Journal your requests to these Divine Beings and love your life.

23

SING FOR FREEDOM AND BLESSINGS WITH ARCHANGEL SANDALPHON AND THE BLUE FLAME ANGELS

Feel your freedom with the Blue Flame Angels. List your Blessings with Archangel Barachiel, who brings Heaven to Earth. Bring in Archangel Sandalphon to help you sing your freedom and blessings. Write your songs here using your creative imagination and Archangel Gabriel. Sing along aloud or to yourself with your Archangels and Blue Flame Angels. Have fun and bring childlike enthusiasm and Harmony to this Music of the Angels.

24

BRING IN ST. MARTIN, ARCHANGEL RAPHAEL AND ARCHANGEL SANDALPHON FOR AN IMAGINATION CREATION OF FORTUNE

Bring in St. Martin, the Saint who helps people bring in abundance, Archangel Raphael, and Archangel Sandalphon for an imagined creation of Fortune. Visualize as St. Martin stands with you and shimmers you with energetic golden coins. Get excited and feel them gently floating down all around you. Feel your abundance. Smile as Archangel Raphael has your back and Archangel Sandalphon stands facing you. As all these divine beings shimmer, an emerald angel sparkles around you. Write any messages you get.

SING SELF LOVE SONGS WITH ARCHANGEL HANIEL AND ARCHANGEL SANDALPHON

Archangel Haniel is the Divine Archangel of Love. Relax and feel your heart area sparkle with Pink Angelic light as you are charged with more self-love. Allow Archangel Sandalphon to join this party and help you create self-love songs and poems to write in your journal. Feel how loved and supported you are by all the Angels, Saints, and your benevolent Ancestors.

BLESSINGS

May the Divine Creative Force that Moves and Creates the Universes Bless and Enhance Every Wish You Ever Conceived that is for the Highest Good of All Involved. May Joy, Peace, and Purpose Be Yours all the Days of your Lives. Through All Time Space and Dimensions. So, Mote, it Be, and So It Is. I hope this book helps you in wonderful ways and radiates out to a gorgeous life for you and yours. May you always Be Blessed and Highly Favored.

Kim Caldwell, creator of the Archangelology Book and Audio Series

REFERENCES

Ascended Masters. Ascended Masters Speak on Angels (Saint Germain Foundation Printing.)

Diana Cooper. The Archangel Guide to Ascension: 55 Steps to Light. (Hay House Inc.)

Matias Flury. Downloads From The Nine: Awaken As You Read. (Matias Flury 2014).

MORE OFFERINGS

Visit https://archangelology.com to discover more Archangels and Super Power Saints

Each of the following books has a matching audio filled with healing music.

Archangelology Michael * Protection

Archangelology Raphael * Abundance

Archangelology Camael * Courage

Archangelology Gabriel * Hope

Archangelology Metatron * Well Being

Archangelology Uriel * Peace

Archangelology Haniel * Love

Archangelology Raziel * Wisdom

Archangelology Zadkiel * Forgiveness

Archangelology Jophiel * Glow

Archangelology Violet Flame * Oneness

Archangelology Sun Angels * Power

Archangelology Moon Angels * Magnetism

Archangelology Sandalphon * Harmony

Archangelology Orion * Expansion

The items below come in book only

Archangelology * Archangel Journaling

Archangelology * Archangel Breath-Tap Book

How Green Smoothies Saved My Life Book

Activate Your Abundance Book and Audio Program

The rest of the items below are available in Audio Format

Archangelology*Mary Magdalene*Feminine Divine Audio

Archangelology * Breath-Tap Super Power Saints Volume 1 Audio

Archangelology * Breath-Tap Super Power Saints Volume 2 Audio

Regeneration Meditations * Switchword Series with Solfeggio Frequencies audio

Radiating Divine Love * Switchword Series with Solfeggio Frequencies audio

Love Charm * Switchword Series with Solfeggio Frequencies audio

Dragon Sun Grounding Meditations * Cosmic Consciousness Series audios

Sweet Moon Sleep Meditation * Cosmic Consciousness Series

Enchanted Earth Sacred Geometry * Cosmic Consciousness Series audios

PLEASE WRITE A HELPFUL REVIEW

If you enjoyed this book please give a positive review so others may find it as well. And may blessings come back for your help.

Thank you so much. May you always be Blessed and highly favored.

Kim

Made in the USA
Columbia, SC
28 July 2024

39459514R00061